KidCaps' Presents
The Construction of the Erie Canal:
A History Just for Kids

KidCaps is An Imprint of BookCaps™
www.bookcaps.com

© 2012. All Rights Reserved.

Table of Contents

ABOUT KIDCAPS 3

INTRODUCTION 5

CHAPTER 1: WHAT LED UP TO THE CONSTRUCTION OF THE ERIE CANAL? 8

CHAPTER 2: WHY DID THE CONSTRUCTION OF THE ERIE CANAL HAPPEN? 11

CHAPTER 3: WHAT HAPPENED DURING THE CONSTRUCTION OF THE ERIE CANAL? 15

CHAPTER 4: WHAT WAS IT LIKE TO BE A KID DURING THE DAYS OF THE ERIE CANAL? 20

CHAPTER 5: HOW DID THE CONSTRUCTION OF THE ERIE CANAL END? 24

CHAPTER 6: WHAT HAPPENED AFTER THE CONSTRUCTION OF THE ERIE CANAL? 26

CONCLUSION 30

About KidCaps

KidCaps is an imprint of BookCaps™ that is just for kids! Each month BookCaps will be releasing several books in this exciting imprint. Visit are website or like us on Facebook to see more!

Introduction

Johnny was a hoggee. Do you know what a hoggee was? A hoggee was the person, often a young boy, who walked with the horses and mules that pulled boats and barges through the Erie Canal. You can see a picture of one at the beginning of this handbook. What do you think it would have been like to be a hoggee? Let's catch up with Johnny as he walks with his family's mules one summer night.

Johnny was ten years old, and he was sitting on the back of a mule. He held the reins in one hand and a thick rope connected to the mule's harness in the other. Next to his mule was another, and they walked, side by side, along the banks of the canal. Each of the mules had a rope attached to it, and the ropes (about 100 feet long) were attached to a barge floating in the water behind him. Normally, he wasn't allowed to lead the mules, but at night, when the whole family was asleep, and there wasn't a lot of traffic on the canal, Johnny's dad let him be the hoggee. It wasn't easy being the only one awake when everyone else was sleeping, and sometimes even Johnny fell asleep right there on the mule. Most of the time it didn't matter: the mules were so well trained that they would keep right on walking down the path without anyone to tell them that they had to.

Johnny had never known any other way of life then living on the Erie Canal. His mother had given birth to him and his little brothers and sisters right there on the barge. Like the rest of the canal kids, Johnny went to school during the winter when the canals froze over. But during the rest of the year, he worked hard with his family taking things back and forth from New York City up the Hudson to Albany, then onto the Erie Canal all the way to Buffalo, on Lake Erie. When they went east on the canal, from Buffalo to Albany, and then down the Hudson to New York City, they normally carried crops from Ohio, like wheat and corn. When they went west, they often carried manufactured goods from the factories in New England. Sometimes, they even carried passengers one way or the other.

Johnny loved living on the Erie Canal. He got to meet so many fascinating people and see new places. Would you have liked to have lived like Johnny did?

In the mid to late 1800s, thousands of people depended on the Erie Canal for their livelihoods. Some people, like Johnny and his family, worked on the barges. They would load up their boats with products and passengers and take them from one end of the canal to the other. In order to get their barges to their destination as quickly as possible, they would run twenty four hours a day. Sometimes, the young boys (like Johnny) would be in charge of leading the animals at night while their fathers and older brothers would do so during the day.

All along the route of the canal, towns appeared and specialized in selling food and clothing to those travelling on the canal. The cities of Buffalo and New York City grew and became prominent in early America.

Now, you might be asking yourself why those people back then decided to build a long canal (finally measuring over 360 miles) instead of just using trains or trucks. Well, remember that life back then was different from the type of life we enjoy today. In fact, cars hadn't even been invented yet. As we will see, building a canal seemed like a crazy idea at the time, but it ended up being the smartest thing that they could have done.

In this handbook, we are going to be answering some interesting questions. Let's enjoy a bit of a preview here. First off, what led up to building the Erie Canal? In that section, we will be learning about the economic and social things that were happening in the United States at the time. Remember, we are talking about a country that was only about 30 years old which meant that everyone, including the President, was kind of figuring out what it meant to be a country and what it meant to be in charge of your own future. We will also see how some things that happened in England affected what people in the United States wanted to do.

Then, we will look at why the Erie Canal was built. Did you know that the Erie Canal wasn't just built to make a few people rich? This new canal helped to solve some fights and prevent rebellion from some of the farmers in the Midwest. What's more, the construction of the Erie Canal was closely related to something called "Manifest Destiny". Have you ever heard that term before? We will be having a closer look at it later on.

After that, we will take a few minutes and see what happened during the construction of the Erie Canal. It wasn't just like digging an enormous ditch: they had to make the boats go higher and lower! In fact, to get from New York City to Buffalo, the barges and boats would have to rise about 600 feet! How do you make a boat rise 600 feet? We will see the fascinating technology used. Then, we will learn about the difficulties faced by the men building the canal, such as terrible diseases and towering trees.

Once the canal was built, we will have a look at what it was like to be a kid working on it. We will sit alongside hoggees like Johnny who lived their lives on the shallow waters of the canal.

After that, we will learn how the construction of the Erie Canal was finally finished and what some of the immediate effects were for the people of the United States. Did you know that some people thought that the whole idea was a waste of time and money? How do you think they felt when they saw the first barges loaded with grain sail into New York Harbor? Do you think they felt kind of silly and embarrassed?

Finally, we will see some of the long term effects of this special canal, including how it is being used today almost two hundred years after its completion. Would you be surprised to know that some people still send their goods on the Erie Canal? Why not use trucks or trains? We will find out.

The construction of the Erie Canal, as we will see, marked a real turning point in American history. It was a time when Americans started to use their imaginations to accomplish the impossible and when they began to try to solve their own problems. Are you ready to learn more? Then let's start with the first section.

Chapter 1: What Led Up to the Construction of the Erie Canal?

As you already know, the original thirteen colonies (stretching from New Hampshire in the north to Georgia in the south) were all on the eastern coast of the land that became the United States. After the Revolutionary War had been fought the American people were interested in continuing to settle the land to the west- but there was one problem. The thirteen colonies and the land to the west were separated by a range of mountains called the Appalachian mountain range. Although people could travel back and forth over the mountains, it was hard to take goods from one side of the mountains to the other.

By the late 1700s, there were lots of farmers living in the Midwest growing different types of grains. However, because they were on the other side of the Appalachian mountain range, it was hard for them to send their grain to the colonies. Also, they couldn't always get the things that they needed from the factories in New England. For some time, the Port of New Orleans had been used as a way to bring things in and out of the Midwest, but French and Spanish occupation of the city made it difficult, sometimes for years at a time, to transport things effectively. A better way had to be found.

In the country of England, the industrial revolution had already begun. Inventors were using machines to run factories, and more and more materials were being moved from one place to another all across England. In England, they faced the same problems as the Americans: how to move large amounts of goods and people from one place to another. Specifically, the factories needed coal to power the large steam engines that were used to make all of the machines work.

An amazing solution to this problem was created in 1769, with the construction of the Bridgewater Canal. Originally built to transport coal from the mines to the large city of Manchester, the 41 mile long canal was a exciting piece of technology. When some Americans saw the canal, they thought: "Why, we can do that too!" However, as you may recall, any canals built in the United States would have to be a whole lot longer than the Bridgewater. Instead of being only 41 miles long, it would have to be about 363 miles long. Could they do it?

A picture of some boats on the Bridgewater Canal today.[1]

Well, the amazing thing about building a canal is that it would not have to be deep. In fact, the Erie Canal was only dug to be about four feet deep. That was deep enough for a barge carrying a lot of cargo. How much cargo could fit on one boat? According to one source, "these boats were designed to carry bulk cargoes of raw materials and manufactured goods. Some of these boats could carry as much as 230 tons of cargo."[2] 230 tons

---

[1] Image source: http://en.wikipedia.org/wiki/File:Worsley_packet_house_closeup_large_image.jpg

[2] Quote source: http://www.canals.org/siteimages/NSF_Building_Americas_Canal

Chapter 2: Why Did the Construction of the Erie Canal Happen?

Although everyone was excited by the Bridgewater Canal built by England in 1769, it wasn't until 1817 that permission was given by the New York State Legislature for work to begin on the Erie Canal. Why did so much time pass, even though a lot of people wanted a canal? Well, as we already mentioned, even though a lot of people wanted a canal, it seemed too difficult to accomplish because of the distance involved, the differences in elevation between the Hudson River and Lake Erie, and because of the enormous cost ($7 million). However, in 1791, something happened that scared a lot of Americans and made them want to find a solution to the east-west transportation problem quickly. What was that historic event? We call it the "Whiskey Rebellion." Let's learn more.

As we saw earlier, there were lots of grain farmers in the Midwest growing things like corn and wheat. However, it was slow, difficult, and expensive to transport the grain that they grew back east. How much time and effort was it to ship grain across the Appalachian Mountains? To help us get an idea, think about this: "In 1812, it took a six-horse team 18-35 days to transport 3,000 pounds of cargo by wagon from Pittsburgh to Philadelphia."[3] If it took so much time and effort to take considerable a distance of only about 300 miles, what about crossing an entire mountain range?

Because it was difficult to make any money selling their crops to those living in the east, many farmers thought that instead of

[3] Quote source: http://www.canals.org/siteimages/NSF_Building_Americas_Canals_Curriculum.pdf

risking their crops rotting on the way to be sold, it would be better to take them and turn them into whiskey. Do you know what whiskey is? Whiskey is a type of alcohol that can be made using corn, wheat, and other types of grains. Whiskey doesn't go sour, and it is pretty expensive. In fact, some farmers began to use whiskey as a form of money because no one was buying their crops. For a while, everything was going well. Then, in 1789, the new U.S. Constitution was approved and new laws on taxation took effect soon after. One of the laws specifically taxed whiskey and other types of alcohol. How did the western farmers respond?

They were exceedingly angry. Because of the poor transportation situation, they could not sell their crops. If they didn't want to lose money, they would have to turn them into whiskey, but now they would have to pay a tax. For those who were paid in whiskey as a kind of money, they now had to pay an income tax that no one else had to. The farmers felt that they were being taxed without local representation, the same thing that they had fought the Revolutionary War in order to stop from happening. In fact, some of the farmers who were being taxed were Revolutionary War veterans. When the farmers and residents refused to pay the tax, President Washington sent troops to the area to put down the rebellion.

A local tax collector is carried out of town during the Whiskey Rebellion.[4]

Although that particular rebellion ended relatively peacefully, it was clear that the problem of transportation needed to be solved. Otherwise, there would be more "Whiskey Rebellions" in the future. That was something that no one wanted to happen.

Another of the factors that finally made Americans agree to build a canal was that term we mentioned in the introduction: "Manifest Destiny." Do you know what that term means? Manifest Destiny was something used by politicians and by the people in general to describe what the future of the United States should be. They felt that the United States was destined to cover all of the land between the Atlantic Ocean and the Pacific Ocean. So, it seemed only natural that there exist some way of transporting goods back and forth between those living in the east and those living further west.

This idea of Manifest Destiny would eventually motivate the American people to take all sorts of risks and to make all kinds of momentous decisions. For example, it was this belief that moved President Jefferson a few years after the Whiskey Rebellion to purchase a large piece of land called the Louisiana territory and to send Meriwether Louis and William Clark to explore the new territory and to push forward all the way to the Pacific.

Manifest Destiny would later move people to go west. However, how could they go and settle new areas if there was no way of making a living once they got there? How could they raise crops if there was no way to get them to the people who wanted them? How could they open up new territories if there were no sure way of getting tools, medicine, and other supplies from the factories in New England? The belief in Manifest Destiny was strong, but it required practical thinking to make it a success.

---

[4] Image source: http://en.wikipedia.org/wiki/File:Whiskey_Insurrection.JPG

Someone had to develop some sort of system of transportation to bring the east closer to the west.

So what did we learn in this section? We learned that although people had been interested in building canals for some time a few factors actually made them become more serious about it in the early 1800s. For example, because of transportation problems farmers turned their crops into whiskey, but then they were heavily taxed later on, leading to the Whiskey Rebellion. Although that particular rebellion did not turn into a large war, it did show that a solution needed to be found.

Also, we learned about Manifest Destiny. Do you remember what that term means? It refers to the belief that the United States was destined to cover all of the land from the Atlantic to the Pacific Oceans. However, in order to support the new colonists and to help them stay in contact with the rest of the country, some sort of canal would have to be built.

The country was ready for a great idea and for a group of men to make it happen. In the next section, we will learn about the actual planning and construction of the Erie Canal.

Work began on July 4, 1817, and the first fifteen miles of the canal were opened in 1819. However, work was going a lot slower than they had planned. What was the problem? There were so many trees in the way that had to be removed one by one. How did the workers do it? They would first cut the tree down and then use a chain attached to a spinning wheel to pull the trunk out of the ground. A group of about three men working this way could take care of one mile per year.

The work could go faster if only there were more workers. But where could they find them? As if in answer to their question, thousands of immigrants, mainly from Ireland, arrived during the next few years to help with the project. They divided into teams and started digging. Using machines pulled by horses, they scraped away large section of dirt until they hit rock. Then, they used gunpowder to blast away the sections of rock that were in their way. Using gunpowder in this way was a pretty new thing to do and sometimes they ended up accidentally blowing pieces of rock onto the roofs of nearby houses!

What did they do with all the dirt that they dug out of the ground? It was piled alongside the canal to create a "towpath", the place where the hoggees and the horses would walk while pulling the boats and barges through the canal.

A clay mixture was placed on the bottom of the canal to make it waterproof, and the sides were covered with cement. While the workers tried keep the canal close to existing rivers in some places, they didn't want to worry too much about crossing strong currents and rapids. So they would build aqueducts to move the boats across rivers and gorges.

Do you remember one of the major challenges of building a canal from Albany on Hudson River to Buffalo on Lake Erie? There was a difference of elevation of about 600 feet, not counting some of the hills along the way. After surveying the land, look at the picture below to see how many times the boats would have to be raised and lowered in order to make their journey.

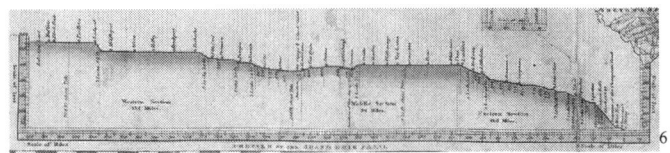

Can you see all of the times that the boats went up and down? How can you make water go up or down? Well, they decided to use the same technology that had been used in England: a system of locks. Do you know what a lock is? A lock is a chamber built as part of a canal where the water inside can be raised or lowered. For example, if the boat needs to go to a higher elevation, then it will enter into the lock and the doors behind it will be closed. Water will be pumped into the chamber, and the boat will rise to the level of the connecting river above it. Then, another set of doors will be opened, and the boat will leave. The same process is used for a boat that needs to be lowered; only in that case water is removed instead of added. You can see a picture of some locks below:

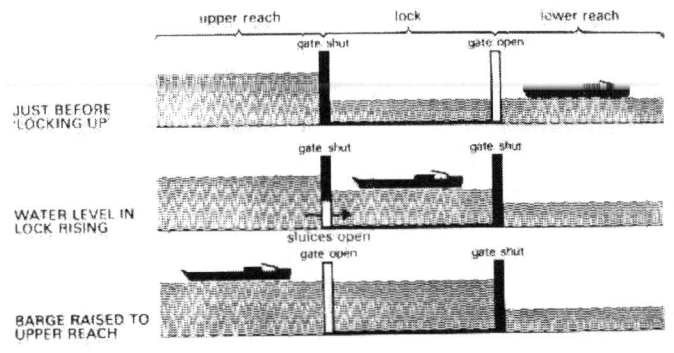

---

[6] Image source: http://en.wikipedia.org/wiki/File:1832_Erie_Canal.jpg

[7] Image source: http://www.schoolshistory.org.uk/IndustrialRevolution/transport/canals.htm

As you can see, a lot of thought and planning went into the design and construction of the Erie Canal.

However, tragedy struck when the builders reached Montezuma Marsh to the west of Syracuse in New York. Because of the hot weather and the swamp conditions, the mosquitos in the area were active. As they bit the workers, many of them began to get sick with what they called "swamp fever" (probably Malaria). Over 1,000 men died before work was halted. They decided to return to that area during the winter, when the mosquitos weren't flying around and biting everyone.

It was a real tragedy because everyone was trying so hard to keep the project just as safe as possible. However, the rest of the men did not lose their spirit, and they kept pushing forward in order to finish the canal. They reached their goal on October 26, 1825, and the project had cost $7 million, just as they had planned for. The entire state of New York took a day to celebrate the wondrous accomplishment. In fact, a series of cannons was placed along the shore, starting in Buffalo, and one after another fired their cannons all the way to New York to celebrate the completion of the canal. A little later, Governor Clinton made the ten-day journey to New York City on a barge and poured some of the water from Lake Erie into New York Harbor.

That was a pretty exciting time to be alive. The American people were able to accomplish what no one thought they could! This is especially incredible when we realize that there weren't really schools for teaching how to make canals and roads back then. In fact, Jesse Hawley, the man who convinced the Governor to move forward with the Erie Canal project wasn't even educated in these things; he just taught himself and the workers learned as they went.

So, what did we learn in this section? We learned that the first attempt to build a canal from the Potomac River to the Ohio River Valley was not successful but that a later attempt by Jesse Hawley was. The construction lasted from July 4, 1817 and lasted until October 26, 1825. The canal itself went from Buffalo to Albany, and had fifty locks to change the height of the boats as they passed over the land. It was truly an engineering marvel.

What do you think it would have been like to be alive back then? Let's find out more.

Chapter 4: What Was It Like to Be a Kid During the Days of the Erie Canal?

Can you imagine living and working on the Erie Canal? What do you think your daily schedule would have been like? Do you think you would have had friends, or do you think that you would have felt lonely? Let's look more at what it was like to be a kid during the time when the Erie Canal was being used the most, during the 1830s and the 1840s.

After the Erie Canal was built, lots of people started to think about how it could change their lives. For example, grain producers living in the Midwest thought about how they could get their grain up to the canal so it could be taken to Albany and New York. Merchants in Albany and New York wanted to know how to get those Midwest grains into their stores. The towns that were built along the shores of the Erie Canal wanted to know how they could make some money from all this grain going back and forth. Someone was needed who could travel from one end of the canal to the other, carrying grain, people, mail, and other goods to all the people who wanted them.

A group of businesspeople decided that it would be a nifty idea to start putting canal barges on the Erie Canal. During most of the year, the barges would just go back and forth across the canal, carrying all sorts of things. Although some canal barges were owned by giant companies, others were owned by small families. In fact, the families didn't just own the barges- they lived on them! The family might have four, five, or even six kids, all of whom helped with the work. The boys would help to load and unload the goods while the girls would help to wash the clothes and to cook the food.

When they were fully loaded, the canal barges tried to run twenty four hours a day so that they could get their cargo to their destination as quickly as possible. The hoggees would normally take turns walking with the animals, and they usually had two or three teams of animals that they took turns with so that none of them got too tired.

Putting a donkey back onto the barge so that it can rest.[8]

Can you imagine being like Johnny, riding on the back of a donkey, looking up at the stars, and seeing the dark shapes of houses pass by as you ride by them? It's kind of weird to be the only one awake, when everyone else is sleeping, but the hoggees had to get used to it. In fact, nighttime was a terrific time to work because there was less traffic.

On the Erie Canal, it wasn't always just serious people trying to carry cargo who used the waters. There were also barges and boats full of people who just wanted to go have some fun on the water. As the boats full of people went sailing by, sometimes they came across bridges that crossed the canal, and the captain of the boat would yell out "low bridge" and everyone would have to duck their head. If someone was standing on the roof of

---

[8] Image source: http://www.youtube.com/watch?v=V7oNKkYFZm8

the barge or if they forgot to duck, they would get knocked down into the water below! As a kid who always worked on the canal, you can be sure that you would laugh plenty at the tourists who forgot where they were.

On hot days, you could always jump into the water and go for a dip. Remember, the canal was only about four feet deep, which means that you could probably almost touch the bottom with your toes if you tried. Would you have to be scared of the boat leaving you behind? Not at all. In fact, there was a speed limit of about 4 mph on the Erie Canal. The speed limit was to make sure that the boats did not mess up the clay bottom, but it also made sure that there were not too many serious accidents and that in case you fell off or wanted to go for a swim, then you could get right back on the boat without too many problems.

During the summer, you would work hard with your family. The families who had barges on the Erie Canal made a lot more than people who had other types of work, but that was because they worked so hard and so much. But when the weather got cooler, most barges would look for a place to take their boats out of the canal. After all, when the water froze, the ice might ruin the wood.

Wintertime meant school for the canal children. You would get into a big, crowded schoolhouse with a wood burning stove, and you would listen to your teacher talk about different subjects, kind of like you still do today. However, back then, it wasn't strange for lots of kids, even little ones and big ones, to be in the same classroom together- because there was only one classroom! Do you think you would have felt weird being in school with kids of all ages? Although wintertime meant no work for the family and school for the kids, a frozen canal did make a perfect place for ice-skating and for having fun. Everyone, kids and adults together, liked to play games and have races on the ice.

The most exciting part of being on the Erie Canal was going through the locks. Do you remember what a lock is? A lock is a little chamber with doors on each side. Inside the chamber, water is either added or taken away in order to make a boat rise to a higher level or go down to a lower one. At the locks, sometimes there were crowds of people gathered just to watch the process. Would you have liked to have been sitting on a boat that was in a lock, with everyone waiting to see what it was like? Would you have felt kind of proud?

A lot of locks had towns built around them where barges and boats could stop to buy supplies, make friends, and even rest a little. It was a marvellous time to meet new kinds of people. As a kid, what kind of people could you expect to have met on the Erie Canal? You could have met the children of immigrants, like the ones from Great Britain who helped to build the canal. Being in the North, where slavery was gradually being made illegal, you could even have met African-American kids just like you, living and working with their families.

Although it was hard work to be a hoggee, you may have actually grown to love the life on the water- as long as you didn't get seasick, that is!

Chapter 5: How Did the Construction of the Erie Canal End?

As we saw earlier, there was a whopping celebration when the construction of the canal was finished. Cannons along the shores lined up and fired of a series of shots, all the way from one end of the canal to the other. Just on time and for the amount of money that they said it should cost, the hardworking men of the crew had finished the Erie Canal. However, there were some problems that still needed to be solved.

First off, there were leaks in different parts of the canal. As you can probably imagine, if all of the water leaked out of the canal, there would be serious problems. It could even damage the lands and houses near the canal. So a recently invented material was put to excellent use: hydraulic cement. Do you know what hydraulic cement is? It is a type of cement that can harden underwater. By putting it over the areas that were leaking, the water drips stopped.

Boats that travelled too quickly through the canal were stirring up the clay bottom and eroding it, making the canal weaker. Like we saw earlier, the solution was to set a speed limit of 4 mph along the entire canal route. Then, there was another problem discovered: too many people wanted to use the Erie Canal at the same time, and they wanted to carry bigger loads through it. The builders had no idea that their canal would become so popular and that it would make so many people happy. How could they solve this problem? Well, only about fifteen years after the original Erie Canal had been completed, the state of New York had to start making plans on how to make it bigger. Can you imagine that? After the canal had been made deeper and wider, it seemed to solve the problem for a while.

Making the canal bigger kept everyone happy for a while.[9]

Then, there was the question of how to pay for the expansion that the canal had needed each year. It was decided that tolls would be collected along the route until the project had paid for itself. This happened in 1882, and the tolls were cancelled from that point on.

The initial construction and expansion of the canal had achieved a lot, but as we will see, there were more changes to come.

---

[9] Image source: http://www.frontdoor.com/city-guide/cleveland-oh-usa/ohio-and-erie-canal-ohio-s-first-great-infrastructure-project

Chapter 6: What Happened After the Construction of the Erie Canal?

After the Erie Canal was built thousands of people got jobs building boats, maintaining the canal, shipping materials, and taking care of the people who needed help along the way. It gave farmers in the Midwest the chance to sell their product, and it gave merchants a chance to sell farm-fresh foods to their customers. Everybody was happy.

However, the Erie Canal had even larger effects that were felt across the entire nation. For example, until the canal was built, there were several cities on the East coast that were all trying to be the most prominent port. For example, we already saw how Washington D.C. tried to become the first city with a canal, even though that project didn't accomplish everything that George Washington wanted it to. Philadelphia, Boston, even Richmond would have all loved to see the economic advantages that New York City saw. New York City became the largest and most prominent port on the east coast. It became the place to go to get fresh food, and everyone who wanted to travel west or to sell their products there had to go to New York.

The construction of the canal also helped people to realize their dreams and to live out their "manifest destiny". Remember, a lot of people thought that the most noteworthy thing for the American people was to move west. Why? Well, things on the east coast were getting crowded. Not every person could have a tremendous farm like they wanted. Also, on the east coast, food wasn't always that fresh. Once the canal was built, the United States saw a large shift of people leaving the cities and moving to "rural" areas for the first time in its history. Do you know what the word "rural" means? It refers to anywhere that is outside of large cities and towns.

Can you imagine only ever having lived in a large city, and then what it was like to pack up your bags, climb onto a canal barge, and start a new life? For many Americans, the Erie Canal was their ticket out west. The Erie Canal would take them as far west as the Great Lakes and the Ohio River Valley. From there, some stayed, and others continued further west past the Mississippi.

The first expansion of the Erie Canal allowed larger and more ships to pass through. However, the whole idea of building canals became so popular that other nearby communities began to build canals of their own and to connect them to the Erie Canal. In fact, the whole area became known the New York State Canal System. But soon, even that wasn't enough. In 1903, New York State Barge Canal was built (costing about $96 million) in order to fit in all the traffic.

For about 100 years, the Erie Canal was one of the most significant routes of transportation in the United States. If anything needed to be taken from one side of the Appalachian Mountain Range to the other, more likely than not it would be taken across the Erie Canal. After all, it cost 90% less to take it on the canal then by any other method.

However, as good as the Erie Canal was, it would not last forever. Why not? America is a country that promotes "capitalism". Do you know what that word means? "Capitalism" is the practice of looking for new ways of doing things and starting new businesses using those technologies to make money. It is one of the things that make the United States a remarkable place. Well, as you can imagine, when some businessmen saw how well the Erie Canal was doing, they wondered how they could make some money too. While some simply chose to buy and sell the goods that were shipped on the canal, others decided to look for a way to replace it altogether. One of the newest technologies and one that did the most to take people off of the Erie Canal was the railroad.

Do you remember what happened to some of the other principal cities on the east coast when the Erie Canal was built? Cities like Baltimore (in Maryland) lost money and people. They wanted to get something for themselves. In order to compete with the Erie Canal, they started something called the Baltimore and Ohio railroad. Can you guess where that railroad went to and from? Like the name says, it started on the east coast in Baltimore and eventually went all the way to Ohio and then to St. Louis, Missouri. While not as cheap as sending things on the canal, the railroad let people send larger and heavier amounts of cargo from east to west and vice versa.

Also, the Baltimore and Ohio (B&O) Railroad was the first "common-carrier" railroad, which meant that anyone could use their services and that the company guaranteed the shipment. No one on the Eric Canal could make a guarantee like that. What's more, trains could get to their destination a whole lot faster, travelling at speeds of around 50 mph while the canal boats only went around 4 mph (plus the waiting time when going through the locks.

As the railroads laid down more and more tracks, moving ever westward, more people preferred the train to the canals. What the effect? Although the Erie Canal had already paid for itself, it still had to be maintained, and some people in the government thought that the money just wasn't worth it anymore. In fact, in 1884, New York State built a railroad of its own called the New York, West Shore and Buffalo Railway. This railroad ran almost the entire route of the Erie Canal. Can you imagine how those working on the Erie Canal felt?

Although it can be difficult when things change, it's not always a bad thing. After all, it was much easier to lay down train tracks than building a canal. And although it was a real unique type of life, living and working on a canal boat, the train just made more sense in a lot of ways. In fact, if it weren't for the train, it would have been a lot more difficult to move people to conquer the Wild West.

Around the turn of the century, in the early 1900s, automobiles were becoming more popular. Around 1914, Henry Ford began experimenting with building cars using an assembly line, which meant that his factory could produce one car every 15 minutes. As more and more cars went onto the roads, and eventually large trucks joined them, both the Erie Canal and the railroads began to suffer. That is what capitalism is all about: using new technology to change the world and to start a new business.

Although the Erie Canal today is mainly used by tourists taking trip on small boats, lately there have been more and more barges on its waters again. Why? The high price of fuel has made shipping some things by canal cheaper than both train and truck. Imagine that: almost two hundred years after it was first designed and built, the canal is being used again to connect people together.

What do you think? Will more and more people start using canals again as transportation? Will the Erie Canal need to be expanded again like it was before? One thing is for sure: we can be glad that the Erie Canal is still around.

Conclusion

Wow! We have learned a lot about the Erie Canal in this report. Did you learn something new, something that you didn't know before? We sure hope so. But before we finish, let's review some of the most salient points.

First off, we learned what led up to building the Erie Canal. Do you remember what some of the principal reasons were for building the canal? Well, the colonies were growing and were running out of space. Also, the technology to build canals had already been used in England, so why not try it in the United States, as well? Although the President at the time had an opportunity to use government money to build the canal, he thought that it was against the law, so the local state government had to do it. Do think they made the right choice?

Then, we looked at why the Erie Canal was built. Did you see how the Erie Canal wasn't just built to make people rich? This new canal helped to solve some fights and prevent rebellion from some of the farmers in the Midwest. Specifically, it stopped the Midwest farmers from getting angry like they did during the Whiskey Rebellion. That was when they had to make their grain into whiskey, but then the whiskey was taxed. The canal let them sell their grain, so everyone was happy. Also, the canal helped Americans fulfill what they saw as their "Manifest Destiny": to move West until reaching the Pacific Ocean.

After that, we took a few minutes to see what happened during the construction of the Erie Canal. It wasn't just like digging a massive ditch because there were trees and rocks in the way. It was only thanks to the hard work of thousands of immigrant laborers that the project was completed. But it was advantageous for the laborers also: they earned about three times as much as they would have back home! Do you remember one of the most difficult parts of building the canal? That's right, they had to make the boats go higher and lower! In fact, to get from New

equals 460,000 pounds, or about 115 cars! How could just two or three mules pull so much weight, when doing so over land would take dozens of animals? Because things weigh less in water, the same animals could pull more weight with less effort. That's what made canals so remarkable.

After seeing what the builders in England were able to accomplish, businessmen in America got excited and wanted to see what they could do. They worked out the math and saw that it would take about $7 million to build the canal. That's a lot of money today, but what about back then? To help us understand, in 1775, only about 30 years before, there was only about $12 million in gold *in the entire nation!* That means that a large project costing $7 million was something so large to almost be silly to even think about. However, as we shall see in the next section, the men who had this brilliant idea did not give up.

So what did we learn in this section? We learned that a lot of people wanted a canal system in the United States because of the Appalachian Mountains. This mountain range made it difficult to ship goods back and forth from the east to the west. Also, Americans at that time wanted to explore the new territories that Great Britain never allowed them to see. There were too many people in the thirteen colonies, and it was getting difficult for everyone to have a house and a farm like they wanted to. But, until there was a sure way for everyone to know that they could ship their crops back east, or they could buy what needed even though they were far away, it didn't seem like a good idea for a lot of people to leave just yet.

The time was right to build a canal, but no one was too sure that it could actually happen. What would have to happen to finally get everyone behind this new project? Let's find out in the next section.

York City to Buffalo, the barges and boats would have to rise about 600 feet. How did they make a boat rise 600 feet? We saw the fascinating technology used: locks that were built all along the canal. Can you explain to a friend or to a family member what a lock is? Can you make a drawing or a model of one? We also learned about the difficulties faced by the men building the canal, such as the swamp fever that killed almost one thousand workers in Northern New York.

Then we had a look at what it was like to be a kid working on the Erie Canal. We sat alongside hoggees like Johnny who lived their lives on the shallow waters of the canal and imagined what it would have been like to live and work on a boat. After that, we learned how the construction of the Erie Canal was finally finished and what some of the immediate effects were for the people of the United States. Finally, we saw some of the long term effects of this special canal, including how it is being used today, almost two hundred years after its completion.

The Erie Canal even changed the way that students are taught in schools. Remember, there actually weren't a lot of men qualified to build a canal, and the ones who finally did it weren't professionals at all. They just worked hard and learned as they went along. After everyone saw how successful they were, they decided to start teaching courses on engineering, building, and design in colleges. The students who went to those schools later helped to conquer the Wild West and to make America the country that made the most use of technology.

Another lesson from the Erie Canal is of the valuable contribution from immigrant workers. Even today, people come to the United States from all kinds of countries to work. Because of the stringer economy and larger amount of jobs, many people can earn much more than they could back home. These immigrants who enter also work in construction, like back then. But many also become lawyers, doctors, and teachers. They work hard, just as people born in America do, to make the community a better place and to care for their families. Like the Erie Canal might never have been built if not for immigrants, the

United States would be different today of not for the thousands who move there ach year to work.

When they needed a way to move goods and people back and forth, the builders of the Erie Canal found a solution to their problem. Although it took lots of hard work, they didn't give up until the project was done. What about you? Will you try to be like them and look for solutions to problems, even to difficult ones? Today, the United States has some pretty hefty problems to deal with, including pollution, drought (not enough water) and try to care for sick citizens. Do you think that you will be able to find solutions to the problems?

Finally, we learned what living in a country that promotes Capitalism actually means. It means that change can come at any time, and that change can affect anyone. However, the change is usually a decidedly good thing, even if some people have to find a different job later on.

The Erie Canal is more than just a story about building a water transportation system: it is a story about America. It shows how problems are solved: by imagination and hard work. It shows how fast change can come: just one hundred years after its construction, the canal had already lost a lot of traffic to trains and trucks. But it also shows how you can never predict the future: the canal is being used again, almost two hundred years later.

What was your favorite part of the handbook? Why not share it with someone and get them read about the Erie Canal too!

The Erie Canal is still being used today. Why not try to visit it with your family?[10]

---

[10] Image source: http://www.nytimes.com/2008/11/03/nyregion/03erie.html

Made in the USA
Middletown, DE
15 November 2016